· MUSIC ·
Folk, Country, and Reggae

Nicolas Brasch

Smart Apple Media

This edition first published in 2005 in the United States of America by Smart Apple Media.

Smart Apple Media
1980 Lookout Drive
North Mankato
Minnesota 56003

Library of Congress Cataloging-in-Publication Data
Brasch, Nicolas.
  Folk, country and reggae / by Nicolas Brasch.
  p. cm.
  Includes index.
  ISBN 1-58340-549-6 (alk. paper)
  1. Folk music—History and criticism—Juvenile literature. 2. Country music—History and criticism—Juvenile literature. 3. Reggae music—History and criticism—Juvenile literature. [1. Folk music. 2. Country music. 3. Reggae music.] I. Title.

  ML3545.B83 2004
  781.64—dc22   2003069485

First Edition
9 8 7 6 5 4 3 2 1

First published in 2003 by
MACMILLAN EDUCATION AUSTRALIA PTY LTD
627 Chapel Street, South Yarra 3141

Associated companies and representatives throughout the world.

Project management by Elm Grove Press
Edited by Helen Duffy
Text design by Judith Summerfeldt Grace
Cover design by Judith Summerfeldt Grace
Photo research by Helen Duffy and Ingrid Ohlsson

Printed in China

Acknowledgements
The author and the publisher are grateful to the following for permission to reproduce copyright material.

Cover photographs: Photodisc (musical instruments); Bruce Postle (left, Willie Nelson, right, reggae musician).

Text photographs: Photodisc (musical instruments), pp. 1 , 8, 9, 20, 21, 23, 29; Bruce Postle, pp. 1 (left, reggae musician), 1 (right, Lee Kernaghan), 3 (top, Smacka Fitzgibbon playing the banjo), 3 (second top, Ani di Franco playing the guitar, Melbourne International Blues Festival, 2003), 3 (third top, string bass player, New Zealand's Ortiz Funeral Directors band, 2003), 4 (from the collection in the Louvre, Paris), 5 (Ani di Franco playing the guitar, Melbourne International Blues Festival, 2003), 7 (Bob Dylan in concert), 9 (Mandawuy Yunupingu of Yothu Yindi, Rod Laver Arena, Melbourne, 2003), 12 (Peter, Paul, and Mary in concert, 1968), 13 (The Seekers in concert), 15 (dawn service, Anzac Day), 16 (string bass player, New Zealand's Ortiz Funeral Directors band, 2003), 19 (Dolly Parton, Melbourne, 1987 concert tour), 20 (Willie Nelson in concert), 21 (Tony Joe White, Melbourne International Blues Festival, 2003), 22 (Johnny Cash in concert); Redferns Music Picture Library, pp. 3 (bottom, copyright Des Willie/Redferns), 10 (copyright Steve Morley/Redferns), 11 (copyright David Redfern/Redferns), 18 (copyright Beth Gwinn/Redferns), 23 (copyright David Redfern/Redferns), 24 (bottom, Barbara Steinwehe/Redferns), 26 (copyright Des Willie/Redferns), 27 (copyright Roberta Parkin/Redferns), 28 (copyright Ian Dickson/Redferns).

While every care has been taken to trace and acknowledge copyright, the publisher tenders their apologies for any accidental infringement where copyright has proved untraceable. Where the attempt has been unsuccessful, the publisher welcomes information that would redress the situation.

Contents

Glossary
When a word is printed in **bold** you can find its meaning in the Glossary on page 31.

Understanding Music

Music has been enjoyed since ancient times.

Main Elements of Music

The main elements of all music are:

dynamics the variation in volume (from loud to soft)

pitch the depth of a sound (whether it is "high" or "low")

rhythm the general pattern or movement of a piece of music, which is created by the length of time between each beat

timbre the tonal quality of a sound

tonality the use of keys in music

Important Musical Terms

chord a combination of two or more musical notes played at the same time

harmony a specific chord or a series of chords

melody a series of musical sounds of different pitch (when you hum the tune of a song, you are usually humming the melody)

texture the thickness of a sound

Music is the arrangement and performance of a combination of sounds that are created by the human voice or by instruments. The ability to turn sounds into music or to create sounds that do not come naturally is something that only humans can do.

The desire to make music is common among all people. It helps us to communicate ideas or emotions and to understand our surroundings and way of life, as well as that of others.

Since ancient times, even isolated communities developed their own forms of music. Different groups used different techniques and instruments to create their own musical sounds.

Music is a creative art form. It also plays an important role in other art forms. Dance and some forms of theater use music to support the action on stage and to help create mood. Music also helps to create atmosphere in films and many television programs.

Music has its own written language, or **score**, made up of symbols and notes. Different musical notes are used to indicate the length of a sound. Notes are represented by the letters A, B, C, D, E, F, and G. These letters or notes are marked on a stave, which is a set of five parallel lines. The position of a note on the stave indicates whether the note is high or low.

Some of the most well-known types of music are:

- classical
- opera
- jazz
- blues
- folk
- country
- reggae
- pop
- rock

This book is about folk, country, and reggae music.

Folk Music

Folk music is simple, traditional music and song that has been handed down from one generation to the next. Early folk songs were not written or recorded, but were passed from one musician to another by playing and singing. These days many folk singers are professional musicians, but others write and perform because they feel they have a story to tell.

The tunes that accompany the stories in folk music are usually simple. They have to be that way so they can easily be learned and handed onto others. Unlike pop and rock music, it is generally the song rather than the performer that is the most important part of folk music. However, some folk artists have achieved worldwide fame.

World Music

Every country has its own folk music. People from Western countries often call folk music from non-Western **cultures** "world music." However, world music is just another form of folk music, passed down by performance rather than by the written word. It usually tells a story about the people who perform it and the land from which they come.

Official Definition of Folk Music

In 1955, members of the International Music Council met in Brazil and came up with an official definition of folk music. Apart from its oral tradition (being passed down by word of mouth), it must "link the present with the past."

History of Folk Music

Ned Kelly, whose parents were Irish, is Australia's most famous bushranger. His life has inspired a number of Australian folk songs. Here he is seen in his last stand against police at Glenrowan in Victoria in 1880.

Most countries have their own form of folk music that goes back hundreds, even thousands of years.

Western Folk Music

In countries such as the United Kingdom, the United States, and Australia, folk music was used to tell stories.

Britain and Ireland

In Britain, the stories were about wars and the hardships that people faced every day. The most famous folk songs are "Greensleeves" (from England), "Cockles and Mussels" (from Ireland), "Will Ye No Come Back Again" (from Scotland) and "When Morning is Breaking" (from Wales).

United States

In the United States, folk songs were particularly popular during the American Civil War in the early 1860s. Folk songs from this era include "Battle Hymn of the Republic," "Dixie," and "When Johnny Comes Marching Home."

Australia

In Australia, many folk songs have dealt with the lives of convicts and outlaws. Songs include "Botany Bay," "Wild Colonial Boy," and "Click Go the Shears." The folk songs have many similarities to those of Ireland, as many early convicts and colonists had Irish backgrounds.

The timeline gives some important events in folk music history between 1928 and 2002. It features performers who are known worldwide.

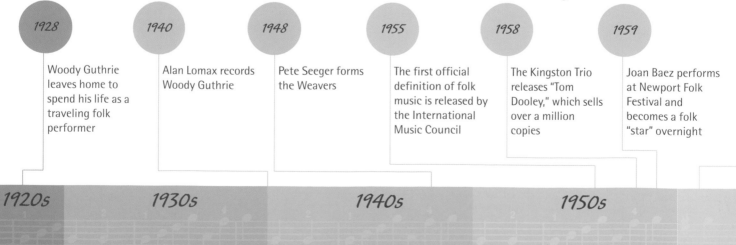

1928
Woody Guthrie leaves home to spend his life as a traveling folk performer

1940
Alan Lomax records Woody Guthrie

1948
Pete Seeger forms the Weavers

1955
The first official definition of folk music is released by the International Music Council

1958
The Kingston Trio releases "Tom Dooley," which sells over a million copies

1959
Joan Baez performs at Newport Folk Festival and becomes a folk "star" overnight

1920s   1930s   1940s   1950s

The Influence of Alan Lomax

One of the most important people in modern folk music history was neither a musician nor a songwriter. His name was Alan Lomax (1915–2002) and he was an American who studied music. He was a **musicologist**.

Lomax spent his life traveling the world, particularly the United States, making tapes of musicians who were playing in the streets, in tiny clubs, even in jails. The one thing these performers had in common was that they were singing about issues close to the heart of the people.

After Lomax recorded the folk songs, he was able to get them played on radio. Many of the musicians whose songs he recorded went on to have successful musical careers simply because Lomax discovered them. Among the folk singers Lomax taped for the first time were Lead Belly, Woody Guthrie, and Muddy Waters.

Folk Music Becomes Popular

Partly because of Alan Lomax and partly because of the politics of the time, folk music became very popular in the 1950s and 1960s. This was particularly the case in the United States, where several folk songs reached the top of the music charts.

Most of these folk songs were protest songs, and they expressed opposition to the Vietnam War, racism, and poverty. Two of the major folk stars who led this protest movement were Bob Dylan and Joan Baez. Some of their songs have become part of the American folk tradition.

In the last 30 years or more, folk music has influenced many musicians. However, it has never managed to reach the same height of popularity that it achieved in the 1960s.

Bob Dylan was one of the leaders of the anti-war protest movement in the 1960s. His song, "Blowin' in the Wind," put into words what many young people were feeling at the time.

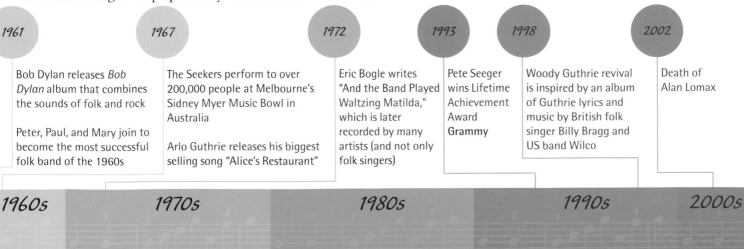

1961
Bob Dylan releases *Bob Dylan* album that combines the sounds of folk and rock

Peter, Paul, and Mary join to become the most successful folk band of the 1960s

1967
The Seekers perform to over 200,000 people at Melbourne's Sidney Myer Music Bowl in Australia

Arlo Guthrie releases his biggest selling song "Alice's Restaurant"

1972
Eric Bogle writes "And the Band Played Waltzing Matilda," which is later recorded by many artists (and not only folk singers)

1993
Pete Seeger wins Lifetime Achievement Award **Grammy**

1998
Woody Guthrie revival is inspired by an album of Guthrie lyrics and music by British folk singer Billy Bragg and US band Wilco

2002
Death of Alan Lomax

1960s　　　1970s　　　1980s　　　1990s　　　2000s

Instruments of Folk Music

The types of instruments used in folk music depend very much on the nationality of the people producing the music, and the environment in which they live. Different groups favor different instruments.

The guitar is the most common string instrument in modern folk music, but the banjo and other versions of the guitar are also used. Some folk musicians even make their own string instruments, the simplest being a wooden box, open on one side, with strings fixed across the opening.

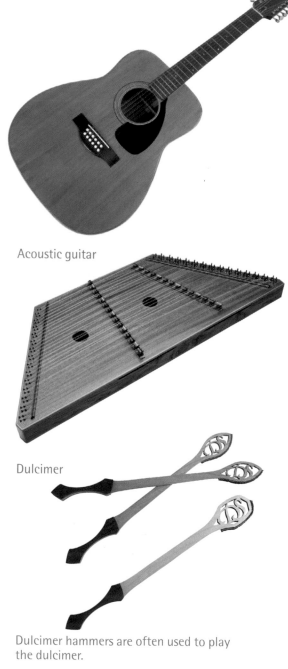

Acoustic guitar

Dulcimer

Dulcimer hammers are often used to play the dulcimer.

Harmonica

Guitar

Most of the best-known folk performers have started their career by learning the guitar, then composing a few of their own songs. Unlike rock musicians, folk singers and folk audiences prefer **acoustic** guitars to electric guitars.

Dulcimer

The dulcimer is a box-like stringed instrument that sits in front of the musician and is played by strumming the strings with the fingers, or small sticks called hammers. The dulcimer was introduced to western Europe in the 1400s, then many countries developed their own versions.

In the United States, the dulcimer was first used in the Appalachian Mountains area. It became known as the Appalachian dulcimer. The sound is gentle and well suited to the tone of folk music.

Harmonica

The harmonica is a popular folk music instrument. Two of the most famous folk (and rock) musicians, Bob Dylan and Donovan, used the harmonica in many of their songs. Sometimes it is used at the same time as the guitar, with the musician using a harmonica holder that hangs around their neck, leaving their fingers free for the guitar.

World Music

Folk music from non-Western countries is sometimes called "world music." This music uses many different instruments.

Talking drum

Africa
African music relies on **percussion** instruments and the most famous is the Kalungu or talking drum. It is shaped like an hourglass and the string or lace that surrounds it can be adjusted to change the sound that it makes.

Asia
The traditional music of many Asian cultures depends heavily on stringed instruments, as well as percussion instruments such as chimes, gongs, and **xylophones**. In China, the *p'ip'a* is popular. It is a type of **lute**.

Middle East
Percussion, stringed, and **wind instruments** all feature in the traditional music of Middle Eastern peoples. One of the wind instruments is an Arabic version of the **bagpipes**.

South America and Central America
Pipes are popular in South and Central America. Some pipes are played by blowing directly into one end, while others are played by blowing across the top of the opening.

Australia
The main instrument used by Aboriginal Australians is the didgeridoo. It is made from a log that has been hollowed out by termites. It is played by blowing into one end.

Lead singer of Aboriginal group Yothu Yindi, Mandawuy Yunupingu, is accompanied here by a musician with a didgeridoo. Yothu Yindi combines rock and roll sounds with traditional Aboriginal songs and performance.

OKAY TEMIZ
Born 1939, Istanbul, Turkey
Full name Okay Temiz
Nationality Turkish
Style Percussion, influenced by traditional Turkish, African, and South American music and western jazz
Recordings include *Drummer of Two Worlds* (1980), *Life Road* (1983), *Magnet Dance* (1995)

KING SUNNY ADE
Born 1946, Oshogbo, Nigeria
Full name Sunda Adeniyi
Nationality Nigerian
Style Juju, which combines guitar rhythms with traditional music of the Yoruba people
Recordings include *Vintage King Sunny Ade* (1970), *Sound Vibration* (1977), *Ariya Special* (1981)

LADYSMITH BLACK MAMBAZO
Year formed/current status 1965 (still performing)
Nationality South African
Style Traditional vocal music called Isicathamiya (pronounced "is-cot-a-me-ya")
Recordings include *Graceland* (with Paul Simon, 1986), *Shaka Zulu* (1987), *Two Worlds One Heart* (1990), *Heavenly* (1999)

Famous Folk Performers

Early folk music was not recorded and it was not until the 1950s and 1960s that some folk music performers became household names. Most of the world-famous folk artists have come from the United States.

Pete Seeger

Born May 3, 1919, New York City, New York, United States
Full name Peter Seeger
Instruments/roles guitar, **vocals**, composer
Hit songs include "Ballad of Harry Bridges" (with the Almanac Singers, 1942), "If I had a Hammer" (1949), "Where have all the Flowers Gone?" (1955)
Hit albums/CDs include *American Industrial Ballads* (1957), *Folk Songs for Young People* (1959), *We Shall Overcome* (1963)
Profile Seeger's mother was a violin teacher and his father a musicologist. Seeger spent years traveling around the United States, learning songs from farmers and other workers. He then performed with the Almanac Singers with Woody Guthrie, then with the Weavers, before going out on his own. His songs were often about political issues such as poverty and the environment.

Woody Guthrie

Born July 14, 1912, Okemah, Oklahoma, United States (died October 3, 1967)
Full name Woodrow Wilson Guthrie
Instruments/roles guitar, vocals, composer
Hit songs include "So Long, It's Been Good to Know Yuh" (1935), "This Land is Your Land" (1940), "Reuben James" (1941)
Hit albums/CDs include *Ballads of Sacco and Vanzetti* (1946)
Profile Guthrie first heard folk music when his mother sang songs that she had learned growing up in Tennessee. He learned the harmonica and began composing his own songs. He left home at 16 and spent the rest of his life "on the road," writing and singing about his experiences. In 1940, his songs were recorded by Alan Lomax. Guthrie inspired many later folk singers and is the most influential modern folk musician. His son, Arlo Guthrie, also became a well-known folk singer.

Pete Seeger

Joan Baez

Born January 9, 1941, Staten Island, New York, United States
Full name Joan Chandos Baez
Instruments/roles guitar, vocals, composer
Hit songs include "There But for Fortune" (1964), "The Night They Drove Old Dixie Down" (1971), "Diamonds and Rust" (1975)
Hit albums/CDs include *Joan Baez* (1960), *Joan Baez in Concert* (1962), *Blessed Are* (1971)
Profile Joan Baez first performed live in the late 1950s in small clubs. In 1959, she played at the Newport Folk Festival, where she made a huge impression. By 1962 she was one of the most popular modern folk musicians. She sang and fought for human rights and peace. She founded the Institute for the Study of Non-Violence.

Joan Baez

Bob Dylan

Born May 24, 1941, Duluth, Minnesota, United States
Full name Robert Allen Zimmerman
Instruments/roles guitar, harmonica, vocals, composer
Hit songs include "Blowin' in the Wind" (1963), "The Times They are A-Changin' " (1964), "Mr. Tambourine Man" (1965), "Maggie's Farm" (1965), "Like a Rolling Stone" (1965), "Lay Lady Lay" (1969)
Hit albums/CDs include *Bob Dylan* (1961), *Freewheelin' Bob Dylan* (1962), *The Times They are A-Changin'* (1964), *Blonde on Blonde* (1966), *Self Portrait* (1970)
Profile Dylan was a successful performer of both folk and rock music. He had an enormous influence on the music of the 1960s, with many young musicians copying his style and writing about important issues. As a songwriter, singer, and performer, his music was used to spark protests against the Vietnam War, poverty, and inequality.

Other Famous Modern Folk Performers

The Almanac Singers (group formed in 1940)
Eric Bogle (born in 1944)
Billy Bragg (born in 1957)
Oscar Brand (born in 1920)
Maybelle Carter (1909–1978)
Len Chandler (born in 1935)
The Chieftains (group formed in 1963)
Donovan (born in 1946)
Arlo Guthrie (born in 1947)
The Irish Rovers (group formed in 1964)
Ralph McTell (born in 1944)
Redgum (group formed in 1973)
Buffy Saint-Marie (born in 1941)

More Famous Folk Performers

The Weavers

Year formed/current status 1949 (disbanded 1963)
Band members Lee Hays (1914–1981), Fred Hellerman (born in 1927), Ronnie Gilbert (born in 1926), Pete Seeger (born in 1919)
Instruments/roles guitars, banjo, vocals, composers
Hit songs include "Goodnight Irene" (1950), "Kisses Sweeter Than Wine" (1951), "On Top of Old Smokey" (1951), "Wreck of the John B" (1952)
Hit albums/CDs include *The Weavers At Carnegie Hall* (1956), *The Weavers At Home* (1958), *Best Of The Weavers* (1959)
Profile Hays and Seeger had previously performed with the Almanac Singers, along with Woody Guthrie. They were the first modern folk artists to have several major hits and their success paved the way for other folk acts. Their strong political views brought them into conflict with some groups. As a result, many of their live bookings were canceled.

Peter, Paul, and Mary. Left to right are "Paul" Stookey, Mary Travers, and Peter Yarrow.

Peter, Paul, and Mary

Year formed/current status 1961 (disbanded 1970)
Band members Peter Yarrow (born in 1938), Noel Stookey ("Paul," born in 1937), Mary Travers (born in 1936)
Instruments/roles guitars, vocals, composers
Hit songs include "If I had a Hammer" (1962), "Blowin' in the Wind" (1962), "Leaving on a Jet Plane" (1967), "Puff (The Magic Dragon)" (1963)
Hit albums/CDs include *Peter, Paul, and Mary* (1962), *In the Wind* (1963), *See What Tomorrow Brings* (1965), *Reunion* (1978)
Profile Peter, Paul, and Mary were the most successful folk band of the 1960s. They had all performed separately in folk clubs and coffee houses before being brought together by promoter Albert Grossman. They produced a smooth, professional sound that won them a far wider audience than most other folk musicians of the time. As a result, several of their songs topped the charts.

The Kingston Trio

Year formed/current status 1957 (disbanded 1967)
Band members Bob Shane (born in 1934), Nick Reynolds (born in 1933), Bob Guard (1934–1991)
Instruments/roles guitars, **ukulele**, vocals, composers
Hit songs include "Tom Dooley" (1958), "Desert Pete" (1963), "The Reverend Mr. Black" (1963)
Hit albums/CDs include *The Kingston Trio* (1958), *From the Hungry i* (1959), *Sold Out* (1960)
Profile The Kingston Trio had a huge hit with their first song, "Tom Dooley." In a few weeks, they went from being performers in small bars to a band with a million-copy hit song. They followed up with several other hits, but serious folk fans considered them a pop act, rather than a traditional folk band. However, other folk bands benefited from their success and popularity.

The Seekers

Year formed/current status 1963 (still performing)
Band members Athol Guy (born in 1940), Keith Potger (born in 1941), Bruce Woodley (born in 1942), Judith Durham (born in 1943)
Instruments/roles guitar, double bass, vocals, composers
Hit songs include "I'll Never Find Another You" (1965), "A World of Our Own" (1965), "The Carnival is Over" (1965), "Georgy Girl" (1967)
Hit albums/CDs include *The Seekers* (1965), *A World of Our Own* (1965), *Live at the Talk of the Town* (1968)

Three members of the Seekers are pictured here (left to right): Judith Durham, Keith Potger, and Bruce Woodley.

Profile This Australian band has split up and reformed several times but was still performing in 2003. They teamed up with English songwriter and producer Tom Springfield in 1964 and immediately hit the top of the charts. In 1965 and 1966, they had the same level of success as the Rolling Stones and the Beatles. They still hold the record for the largest crowd at an Australian concert: more than 200,000 at the Sidney Myer Music Bowl in Melbourne in 1967.

Famous Folk Compositions

Most famous folk compositions have been performed and recorded by many different artists. Sometimes an artist has more success with a song than the original writer or performer, such as Peter, Paul, and Mary's success with the Pete Seeger song, "If I had a Hammer."

Folk Compositions in the Grammy Hall of Fame

There are six folk compositions in the Grammy Hall of Fame. Compositions can only gain admission to the Grammy Hall of Fame 25 years after their first release. The first date is the year of **induction**. The second date is the year of the song's release by the named performer or group.

1989 "This Land is Your Land" (1947)
  Woody Guthrie
1994 "Blowin' in the Wind" (1963) Bob Dylan
1998 "Tom Dooley" (1958) The Kingston Trio
2002 "Goodnight Irene" (1936) Lead Belly
  "Where Have All The Flowers Gone"
  (1964) Pete Seeger
  "Alice's Restaurant" (1967) Arlo Guthrie

"Tom Dooley"

Year written 1800s
Writer Unknown
Performers The Kingston Trio, Frank Warner
This song contributed to the popularity of folk music in the late 1950s and 1960s. It tells of Tom Dula, a Civil War soldier, who was wrongfully hanged for murder in 1868. Frank Warner heard it sung in the 1930s by Frank Proffitt, whose family had passed it down from one generation to the next. Warner got Proffitt to sing it into a tape recorder. The words and music were later published by folk historian Alan Lomax.

"Cockles and Mussels"

Year written 1870s
Writer James Yorkston
Performers Irish Weavers, The Dubliners
Also known as "Molly Malone," this was written as a comic song. It is often associated with Ireland, but was actually written by a Scotsman. Apart from the versions released by the groups named above, the song has been sung by many individual artists, including Burl Ives.

"John Brown's Body"

Year written 1860s
Writer William Steffe (but poet Julia Howe later changed the words and turned it into "Battle Hymn of the Republic")
Performers Sylvia O'Brien, Paul Robeson, Pete Seeger
"John Brown's Body" came from a camp song that was popular in the United States in the early 1860s, at the time of the American Civil War. The words were changed to include references to John Brown, a man who was campaigning to stop slavery.

"Danny Boy"

Year written 1912
Writer Fred Weatherley
Performers Bing Crosby, The Chieftains, James Galway
Written by an Englishman, this is not an Irish folk song as is often thought. Weatherley wrote the **lyrics** in about 1910, and in 1912 put them with the tune "Londonderry Air." "Danny Boy" became a hit.

"Streets of London"

Year written 1969
Writer Ralph McTell
Performers Ralph McTell, The Pogues, Harry Belafonte
This song is based on Ralph McTell's experiences walking around London, and seeing people starving and homeless. The song has been performed and recorded by hundreds of musicians.

"And the Band Played Waltzing Matilda"

Year written 1972
Writer Eric Bogle
Performers Eric Bogle, June Tabor, Archie Fisher
This song is about the Anzac soldiers at Gallipoli and was written after Bogle watched an Anzac Day parade. It has been recorded in Danish, Spanish, French, and Portuguese.

Folk Albums in the Grammy Hall of Fame

There are five folk albums in the Grammy Hall of Fame. The first date is the year of induction. The second date is the year of the album's release by the performer or group.

1998 *Negro Sinful Songs* (1939) Lead Belly
Dust Bowl Ballads, Volumes 1 & 2 (1940) Woody Guthrie
The Weavers At Carnegie Hall (1957) The Weavers
1999 *We Shall Overcome* (1963) Pete Seeger
2003 *In the Wind* (1963) Peter, Paul, and Mary

In Australia, dawn services and parades are a feature of Anzac Day each year on April 25. An Anzac Day event inspired Eric Bogle to write "And the Band Played Waltzing Matilda."

Country Music

Country music is American popular music that developed in the southeastern United States. In the 1920s, it combined with music from the south-west to become country and western music. Country music is simple in form and uses few instruments.

Country music originated from folk songs and ballads sung by British and Irish settlers in the United States. The lyrics usually deal with love, religion, crime, prison, the life of the drifter, or the hardships of living on the land.

Since the 1970s, the appeal of country music has spread worldwide. Now many country artists regularly have hit songs that sell more copies than pop and rock songs.

Country Music Styles
There are many different styles of country music.

Bluegrass
Bluegrass is a fast-paced style of music and bands only use stringed instruments, such as guitars, mandolins, fiddles, string basses, and banjos. In its purest form, the instruments should not be **amplified**.

Cowboy Music
Cowboy music features the gentle strumming of a guitar and the lyrics focus on the joys of life on the range. This music was particularly popular in the 1930s and 1940s.

Honky-tonk
Honky-tonk music introduced amplified instruments to country music. The lyrics tell stories of wild drinking, dancing, and loving, sung to the sound of a steel guitar. While some honky-tonk songs are fast, many are slow and sad, and tell of love gone wrong. These "crying in your beer" sad songs are very much associated with country music.

Western Swing
Western swing music combines country music and jazz. It developed from the 1940s swing style of jazz. Western swing introduced the electric guitar to country music and can also include drums and a brass section.

Rockabilly
Rockabilly, popular in the 1950s, combines country music and rock, and relies heavily on the guitar, bass, and drum.

Nashville Sound
The Nashville sound started as a reaction against the loudness of rock and roll. The Nashville sound puts the emphasis on the lyrics of a song, rather than the music.

New Traditionalist Movement
The new traditionalist movement combined pop and country music in a bid to appeal to younger audiences. It updated the honky-tonk and western swing styles.

BLUEGRASS STARS
Bill Monroe (1911–1996)
Lester Flatt (1914–1979)
Earl Scruggs (born in 1924)
Red Smiley (1925–1972)
Don Reno (1927–1984)
Ralph and Carter Stanley (duo formed in 1946)

COWBOY MUSIC STARS
Carl T. Sprague (1895–1978)
Gene Autry (1907–1998)
Roy Rogers (1911–1998)
Sons of the Pioneers (group formed in 1933)

HONKY-TONK STARS
Ernest Tubb (1914–1984)
Floyd Tillman (born in 1914)
Kitty Wells (born in 1919)
Hank Williams (1923–1953)
Lefty Frizzell (1928–1975)
Tammy Wynette (1942–1998)

WESTERN SWING STARS
Milton Brown (1903–1936)
Bob Wills (1905–1975)

ROCKABILLY STARS
Gene Vincent (1935–1971)
Eddie Cochran (1938–1960)

NASHVILLE SOUND STARS
Eddy Arnold (born in 1918)
Jim Reeves (1923–1964)
Patsy Cline (1932–1963)
Glen Campbell (born in 1936)

NEW TRADITIONALIST STARS
George Strait (born in 1952)
Reba McEntire (born in 1955)
Dwight Yoakam (born in 1956)
Alan Jackson (born in 1958)
k. d. lang (born in 1961)

History of Country Music

Country music developed from English, Scottish, and Irish folk music in the southern United States in the mid-to-late 1800s. Early settlers brought their songs with them and each community had a different style. For example, those from Britain were influenced by British folk music, and those from Ireland by Irish folk music. All wanted to tell their stories through music.

The Grand Ole Opry was established in 1925 to promote country music. It was a place where artists could perform in order to become known.

The timeline gives some important events in country music history between 1922 and 2000.

Early 1900s

By the early 1900s, the various musical styles of the different communities had combined to form a new style. It relied heavily on fiddles, banjos, and guitars and became known as country music. At the same time, good quality stringed instruments became more widely available. As a result, virtually anyone interested in the new form of music could pick up an instrument and begin playing. The music was usually performed at home, in church, or at local functions.

The 1920s

By the mid-1920s, record players had been invented and country musicians were making records. Suddenly, a good country musician could reach far more people than they had ever dreamed of reaching. Before record players, musicians had to "go on the road," touring the country for years and years, in order to become well-known.

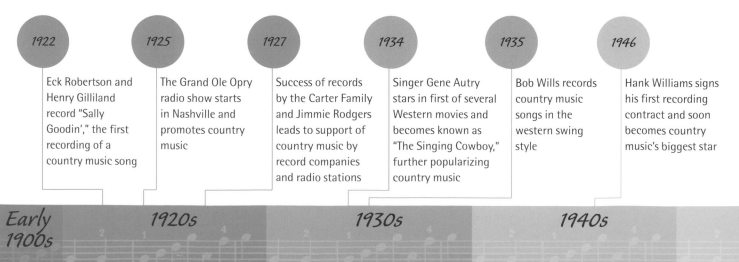

1922
Eck Robertson and Henry Gilliland record "Sally Goodin'," the first recording of a country music song

1925
The Grand Ole Opry radio show starts in Nashville and promotes country music

1927
Success of records by the Carter Family and Jimmie Rodgers leads to support of country music by record companies and radio stations

1934
Singer Gene Autry stars in first of several Western movies and becomes known as "The Singing Cowboy," further popularizing country music

1935
Bob Wills records country music songs in the western swing style

1946
Hank Williams signs his first recording contract and soon becomes country music's biggest star

Early 1900s　　1920s　　1930s　　1940s

The Grand Ole Opry

In 1925, WSM radio in Nashville, Tennessee, began a radio program that focused on country music. Country artists were invited to perform live and their shows were heard by listeners around the United States. The show was called the "Grand Ole Opry" and it still exists. It got its name because it replaced a program called "Grand Opera," and the first host of the show thought that "Grand Ole Opry" made a humorous statement.

The success of the Grand Ole Opry was almost immediate and country music acts all over the country began sending tapes to the radio station in the hope that they would be selected to perform. Even today, young country musicians starting out dream of appearing on the show and becoming big stars.

Nashville

With the success of the Grand Ole Opry, other music businesses began setting up in Nashville to serve the musicians and fans who moved to the city. Since the late 1920s, most aspiring country music stars have headed to Nashville. It is now home to record companies, radio stations, music publishers, and performance spaces, all devoted to country music.

Dolly Parton has won fame as a singer and songwriter. She helped to bring country music to a wider audience by combining country and rock music. She wrote "I Will Always Love You," the theme song to the film *The Bodyguard*, which Whitney Houston sang and made a No. 1 hit worldwide.

Country Music Today

Since the 1970s, country music has regularly featured on popular music charts. Country stars such as Garth Brooks and Reba McEntire know that by combining elements of country and rock music, they can appeal to both markets.

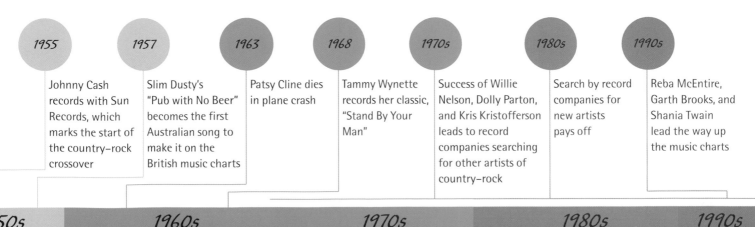

1955	1957	1963	1968	1970s	1980s	1990s
Johnny Cash records with Sun Records, which marks the start of the country–rock crossover	Slim Dusty's "Pub with No Beer" becomes the first Australian song to make it on the British music charts	Patsy Cline dies in plane crash	Tammy Wynette records her classic, "Stand By Your Man"	Success of Willie Nelson, Dolly Parton, and Kris Kristofferson leads to record companies searching for other artists of country–rock	Search by record companies for new artists pays off	Reba McEntire, Garth Brooks, and Shania Twain lead the way up the music charts

1950s   1960s   1970s   1980s   1990s

Instruments of Country Music

Country music relies heavily on stringed instruments, such as the fiddle, guitar, banjo, and string bass, but the harmonica is also favored.

Fiddle and bow

Fiddle

The fiddle sums up country music more than any other instrument. "Fiddle" is just another word for violin. Most forms of country music feature the fiddle. The most famous fiddle song is "The Devil Came Down to Georgia."

Guitar

The guitar is an essential instrument in country music. The acoustic guitar is popular, but many country music bands also have a steel guitar player.

The steel guitar is mounted on legs. It has metal strings that are much further from the **fingerboard** than most other guitars. It has a steel **slide** attached to it, which the musician moves up and down the strings to produce the desired notes. The steel guitar is particularly popular in the slow, "crying in your beer" songs of the honky-tonk style. This is because it can reproduce a sad, mournful sound.

Acoustic guitar

Steel guitar

Willie Nelson, like Dolly Parton and others, helped widen the appeal of country music by mixing country and rock styles. He generally plays an acoustic guitar.

Banjo

The banjo is a very popular instrument in bluegrass country music. It is a five-stringed instrument that originated in Africa. One of the most famous bluegrass songs is "Dueling Banjos," in which two banjo players compete to see who can play the fastest.

String Bass

Country music features the string bass, also known as the double bass. It is like a giant violin and is played standing up. The **bow** is drawn across the front of the instrument. It is common in bluegrass and rockabilly music.

Harmonica

The harmonica or mouth organ is popular with a number of country music performers. It was invented in the early 1800s by a German, Christian Buschmann. It was based on the keys of an organ and consists of a number of reeds placed inside a metal box, with small openings along the edge. It is played by moving it along the mouth and blowing air into, or sucking air out of, the openings.

Some country musicians play the guitar and the harmonica at the same time. They do so by attaching the harmonica to a frame that fits around their neck. Their hands are then free to play the guitar.

Performer Tony Joe White plays the harmonica and guitar at the same time.

Banjo

String bass or double bass

Harmonica or mouth organ

Famous Country Performers

Country music particularly rewards female performers. Patsy Cline, Kitty Wells, Loretta Lynn, Patsy Montana, Tammy Wynette, Dolly Parton, Reba McEntire, and Shania Twain are among the most successful and popular country artists of all time.

Johnny Cash

Johnny Cash

Born February 26, 1932, Kingsland, Arkansas, United States (died 2003)
Full name John R. Cash
Hit songs include "I Walk the Line" (1956), "Folsom Prison Blues" (1956), "A Boy Named Sue" (1969)
Hit albums/CDs include *At Folsom Prison* (1968), *At San Quinten* (1969), *Unchained* (1998)
Profile Known as "The Man in Black" because he only wore black clothes, Cash recorded 1,500 songs and 500 albums and had more hit singles than rock legends such as Michael Jackson and Elton John. He sold over 50 million records throughout his career.

Hank Williams

Born September 17, 1923, Georgiana, Alabama, United States (died 1953)
Full name Hiram King Williams
Hit songs include "Honky Tonkin" (1947), "Lovesick Blues" (1949), "Hey Good Lookin' " (1951), "Your Cheatin' Heart" (1953)
Hit albums/CDs include *Moanin' the Blues* (1952), *Memorial Album* (1953), *Hank Williams Sings* (1955)
Profile Williams started singing as a boy in his church choir and began playing guitar at age seven. He wrote his first song when he was 12 and formed his first band a couple of years later. In the late 1940s and early 1950s, he was country music's biggest star. Fifty years after his death, his recordings outsell many songs by today's top country music performers.

Patsy Cline

Born September 8, 1932, Winchester, Virginia, United States (died 1963)
Full name Virginia Patterson Hensley
Hit songs include "Crazy" (1961), "I Fall to Pieces" (1961), "She's Got You" (1962)
Hit albums/CDs include *Patsy Cline* (1957), *Patsy Cline Showcase* (1961), *Sentimentally Yours* (1962)
Profile Cline won a talent quest in 1957 and appeared on the Grand Ole Opry radio show the following year. Her appearance on the show attracted a lot of interest and at the beginning of the 1960s she was country music's biggest star. She was killed in a plane crash in 1963.

Tammy Wynette

Tammy Wynette

Born May 5, 1942, Itawamba County, Mississippi, United States (died 1998)
Full name Virginia Wynette Pugh
Hit songs include "I Don't Wanna Play House" (1967), "Stand By Your Man" (1968), "D-I-V-O-R-C-E" (1968)
Hit albums/CDs include *Stand By Your Man* (1968), *The Best of Tammy Wynette* (1976), *Anniversary* (1987)
Profile Wynette had moderate success as a singer before being signed to Epic Records by producer Billy Sherrill. With Sherrill's help, she had hit after hit. Her song "Stand by Your Man" is the biggest-selling song by a female country music artist.

The Country Music Hall of Fame

There have been 88 performers inducted into the Country Music Hall of Fame since it was established in 1961. This is a list of the first 20 performers to be inducted, between 1961 and 1972.

Jimmie Rodgers (1897–1933)
Fred Rose (1898–1954)
Hank Williams (1923–1953)
Roy Acuff (1903–1992)
Tex Ritter (1905–1974)
Ernest Tubb (1914–1984)
Eddy Arnold (born in 1918)
James R. Denny (1911–1963)
George D. Hay (1895–1968)
Uncle Dave Macon (1870–1952)

Red Foley (1910–1968)
J. L. Frank (1900–1952)
Jim Reeves (1923–1964)
Stephen H. Sholes (1911–1968)
Bob Wills (1905–1975)
Gene Autry (1907–1998)
Bill Monroe (1911–1996)
Original Carter Family (first recorded in 1927)
Arthur Edward Satherley (1889–1986)
Jimmie H. Davis (1899–2000)

More Famous Country Performers

Glen Campbell

Born April 22, 1936, Delight, Arkansas, United States
Full name Glen Travis Campbell
Hit songs include "By the Time I Get to Phoenix" (1967),
"Wichita Lineman" (1968), "Galveston" (1969),
"Rhinestone Cowboy" (1975)
Hit albums/CDs include *Glen Campbell: Live* (1969),
Glen Travis Campbell (1972), *Reunion* (1974)
Profile Campbell was a backing guitarist for other singers
before playing with the Beach Boys in 1964–65. A string
of **solo** hit singles in the late 1960s made him a star and
earned him his own national television show.

Garth Brooks

Born February 7, 1962, Tulsa, Oklahoma, United States
Full name Troyal Garth Brooks
Hit songs include "If Tomorrow Never Comes" (1989),
"The Dance" (1989), "The River" (1991)
Hit albums/CDs include *Garth Brooks* (1989),
No Fences (1990), *Roppin' the Wind* (1991)
Profile Brooks has increased the popularity of country
music. His style appeals to both country and rock
music fans and he has sold over 80 million records.

Reba McEntire

Born March 28, 1955, Chockie, Oklahoma, United States
Full name Reba Nell McEntire
Hit songs include "Can't Even Get the Blues" (1983),
"One Promise Too Late" (1987), "How Was I to Know" (1997)
Hit albums/CDs include *For My Broken Heart* (1991), *It's Your Call* (1992)
Profile Reba was discovered while singing the American national
anthem at a rodeo and has gone on to sell over 50 million records.

Garth Brooks

Famous Country Compositions

In country music, the songwriters are held in much higher regard than they are in pop and rock music. Although many performers write their own songs, others rely on songwriters to provide them with hits.

"The Devil Came Down to Georgia"

Year released 1979
Writer Charlie Daniels
Performer Charlie Daniels Band
This song highlights the fiddle and has been performed and recorded by many great country fiddle players.

"Honky Tonkin'"

Year released 1947
Writer Hank Williams
Performer Hank Williams
This song set Hank Williams on the road to stardom. It was also a No. 1 hit for his son, Hank Williams Junior, in 1982.

"Crazy"

Year released 1962
Writer Willie Nelson
Performer Patsy Cline
This was the huge hit that made Patsy Cline a country music star. The song's writer, Willie Nelson, is a country music legend.

"Coal Miner's Daughter"

Year released 1970
Writer Loretta Lynne
Performer Loretta Lynne
Lynne wrote this song about her upbringing as a coal miner's daughter. It was later to become the title of a film based on her life.

The Grammy Hall of Fame

The Grammy Hall of Fame was established in 1973. Songs cannot be inducted until 25 years after release. Over 40 country songs have been included. Some of them are listed here.

"Blue Yodel (T for Texas)" (1928) Jimmie Rodgers
"Wildwood Flower" (1929) The Carter Family
"Back in the Saddle Again" (1937) Gene Autry

"Pistol Packin' Mama" (1943) Al Dexter
"I'm So Lonesome I Could Cry" (1949) Hank Williams
"Hey Good Lookin' " (1951) Hank Williams
"Your Cheatin' Heart" (1953) Hank Williams
"Sixteen Tons" (1955) "Tennessee" Ernie Ford
"Crazy Arms" (1956) Ray Price
"Folsom Prison Blues" (1956) Johnny Cash
"El Paso" (1959) Marty Robbins

"He'll Have To Go" (1959) Jim Reeves
"Crazy" (1962) Patsy Cline
"King of the Road" (1965) Roger Miller
"Stand By Your Man" (1968) Tammy Wynette
"Wichita Lineman" (1968) Glen Campbell
"Hello Darlin' " (1970) Conway Twitty
"Help Me Make it Through The Night," (1970) Sammi Smith
"Behind Closed Doors" (1973) Charlie Rich

Reggae Music

Reggae is a popular form of Jamaican music. It developed in the 1960s, drawing on music from the United States and traditional African–Jamaican folk music and ska, a form of dance-hall music. Reggae has a springy, offbeat rhythm, and a laid-back sound.

The Rastafarian Movement

Reggae songs are often political and closely linked to the Rastafarian religion, which celebrates Africa as the home of black Jamaicans. Rastafarians worship the former president of Ethiopia, Haile Selassie.

Styles of Reggae

There are four main styles of reggae: traditional reggae (known simply as reggae), ska, rock steady, and dub.

Reggae

Traditional reggae has a slow, floating rhythm. Audiences sway to the music rather than dance to it. The most famous reggae performer is Bob Marley.

Ska

Ska has a faster, sharper beat than traditional reggae and most bands feature a horn section. It was popular in dance halls of the 1950s. Desmond Decker and Toots Hibbert are among the most famous ska performers.

Rock Steady

Rock steady is a cross between ska and traditional reggae. It has the smoothness of reggae but is still catchy enough to dance to its beat.

Dub

Dub has a very heavy bass sound and very little rhythm section. It is music for listening to rather than dance music.

Great Reggae Artists

Prince Buster (born in 1938)
Desmond Dekker (born in 1941)
U-Roy (born in 1942)
Peter Tosh (1944–1987)
Bob Marley (1945–1981)
Jimmy Cliff (born in 1948)
Eddy Grant (born in 1948)
Big Youth (born in 1949)
Gregory Isaacs (born in 1951)
Sly Dunbar (born in 1952)
Robbie Shakespeare (born in 1953)
Dennis Brown (1956–1999)
Yellowman (born in 1956)
Toots and Maytals (group formed in 1962)
Shaggy (born in 1968)

Reggae bands generally include drums.

Island Records

One person who played a major role in helping reggae become popular worldwide was Chris Blackwell. He was a white Jamaican man who set up Island Records in the 1960s. Blackwell began promoting reggae outside Jamaica.

Even Blackwell could not have imagined the influence reggae would have on countries such as Britain, the United States, and Australia. For a country with less than three million people, this Jamaican music has had a huge influence on other forms of modern music such as rock and jazz.

History of Reggae Music

Reggae started in Jamaica when young Jamaicans, influenced by popular North American music of the mid-1960s, began adding their own sounds and rhythms to traditional African–Jamaican music.

The 1950s

The first form of reggae was ska. It combined a Jamaican sound with American blues, jazz, and rock and roll. In the 1950s, one of the most popular pastimes for young Jamaicans was to hang around disc jockeys who set up sound systems in halls, houses, and even on the streets. The disc jockeys were often record producers and they paid attention to the reaction of the crowd to the music. As a result, the sounds being played changed rapidly.

The 1960s

By the mid-1960s, the ska sound had slowed down a little and the bold brass section had given way to the smoother sound of the keyboards. This was the rock steady style. By the end of the 1960s, this sound had slowed even more and turned into reggae. From this period came the three legends of reggae, Bob Marley, Peter Tosh, and Jimmy Cliff.

Bob Marley, reggae's most famous performer, has produced some of its most famous songs.

The timeline gives some important events in reggae music history between the 1950s and the 1990s.

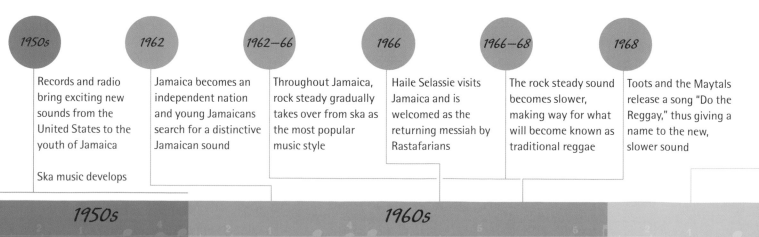

1950s
Records and radio bring exciting new sounds from the United States to the youth of Jamaica

Ska music develops

1962
Jamaica becomes an independent nation and young Jamaicans search for a distinctive Jamaican sound

1962–66
Throughout Jamaica, rock steady gradually takes over from ska as the most popular music style

1966
Haile Selassie visits Jamaica and is welcomed as the returning messiah by Rastafarians

1966–68
The rock steady sound becomes slower, making way for what will become known as traditional reggae

1968
Toots and the Maytals release a song "Do the Reggay," thus giving a name to the new, slower sound

1950s   1960s

Instruments of Reggae Music

Most Western music puts the stress on the first and third beats in each **bar**, but reggae music puts the stress on the second and fourth beats. Several instruments help to create the offbeat rhythm.

Electric bass guitar

Guitar

Unlike most forms of modern music, it is the bass guitar, rather than the rhythm guitar, that dominates the reggae sound. The bass guitar produces a strong rhythm that represents the heart beat.

Drums

In reggae, drums do more than just provide the beat. They give the music life. Reggae drummers follow traditional African music, which suggests that drums communicate with the spirit world. Musicians have to feel the music running through them.

African drums have influenced reggae music. This is an African djembe drum.

Brass Instruments

Ska music, which came before reggae, depends heavily on the saxophone and other brass instruments such as the trombone. In fact, ska is one of the few forms of modern music in which the trombone plays a vital part.

Saxophone

Trombone

1972
Bob Marley and the Wailers sign a record deal with Island Records

1974
Rock star Eric Clapton has a No.1 hit with the Bob Marley song "I Shot the Sheriff"

1975
Bob Marley and the Wailers have a hit single and hit album on the British charts

1981
Bob Marley dies

1990s
Since the 1980s, rock bands and solo performers worldwide have success in blending reggae with their music

1970s   *1980s*   *1990s*

Famous Reggae Performers and Compositions

Three people, Bob Marley, Jimmy Cliff, and Peter Tosh, are responsible for many of reggae's best-known songs.

Peter Tosh

Born October 9, 1944, Grange Hill, Jamaica (died 1987)
Full name Winston Hubert McIntosh
Hit songs include "Legalize It" (1976), "(You Gotta Walk) Don't Look Back" (with Mick Jagger, 1978), "I'm the Toughest" (1978)
Hit albums/CDs include *Catch a Fire* (1973), *Legalize It* (1976), *Equal Rights* (1977)
Profile Tosh was a member of Bob Marley's band, the Wailers, before going solo. Apart from Marley, Tosh is seen as one of the top reggae artists.

Jimmy Cliff

Born April 1, 1948, Somerton, Jamaica
Full name James Chambers
Hit songs include "Wonderful World Beautiful People" (1968), "Many Rivers to Cross" (1970), "The Harder They Come" (1972)
Hit albums/CDs include *Another Cycle* (1971), *The Harder They Come* (1972), *Give the People What They Want* (1981)
Profile Cliff's songs have been recorded by a number of major rock artists.

Bob Marley

Born February 6, 1945, St. Ann, Jamaica (died 1981)
Full name Robert Nesta Marley
Hit songs include "Get Up, Stand Up" (1973), "No Woman No Cry" (1974)
Hit albums/CDs include *Natty Dread* (1974), *Live* (1975), *Exodus* (1977)
Profile Marley is the superstar of reggae and the person most responsible for its success outside Jamaica. He formed the Wailers in 1963 and in the next 18 years, before his death in 1981, he produced many great songs.

"MY BOY LOLLIPOP"

Year released 1964
Writers Johnny Roberts and Morris Levy
Performer Little Millie
This was the first reggae song to be an international hit and the first hit song for Island Records. The success of the song enabled Island Records to promote other reggae artists such as Bob Marley.

"NO WOMAN NO CRY"

Year released 1974
Writer Vincent Ford
Performer Bob Marley
This song was first released as a studio single in 1974. However, it was the live version, performed by Marley in London and released in 1975, that launched him toward international stardom.

"MANY RIVERS TO CROSS"

Year released 1970
Writer Jimmy Cliff
Performer Jimmy Cliff
This is the title song of the soundtrack of *The Harder They Come*, the most famous Jamaican film. The song is considered Cliff's greatest work.

Glossary

acoustic   having a sound made naturally, rather than made louder by electronic means

amplified   made louder by the use of electricity

bagpipes   Scottish reed instrument consisting of a number of pipes attached to a windbag, into which air is blown by the mouth or a bellows

bar   vertical line drawn across the stave in a piece of written music, to separate groups of notes; it also refers to the group of notes between two bars

bow   wooden stick with horse's hair stretched along its length

cultures   groups, communities, or nations, made up of people who share a common way of life

fingerboard   the long, narrow part of the guitar on which the strings are stopped by the fingers

Grammy   the major music award in the United States

induction   election or introduction

lute   stringed instrument with a long neck and pear-shaped body

lyrics   words to a song

musicologist   someone who studies music

percussion   percussion instruments are those that make a loud banging or crashing sound, such as drums, cymbals, triangles, tambourines, and xylophones

score   written copy of a piece of music

slide   the part of a steel guitar that can be moved along the strings to alter the pitch

solo   one single performer, or instrument playing on its own

ukulele   small four-string guitar from Hawaii

vocals   the singing part of a song

wind instruments   instruments that are played by blowing air into a mouthpiece, such as flutes and clarinets

xylophone   wooden instrument with keys arranged like piano keys, which are struck with small sticks called mallets

Index